Jai Publishing
WRITE. RELEASE. HEAL.

Jai PublishingHouse Incorporated
Website: www.jaipublishing.com
Email: info@jaipublishing.com

Printed in the United States of America

ISBN: 978-0-578-64171-3

How To Use This **Planner**

Watch the video at
bit.ly/2020visionplanneroverview

This **Business Planner** belongs to

_____

Two things you are in control of in life are your attitude & your effort.

Your X-It Date: _____

Jennifer King

I designed this **Business Planner** for FRUSTRATED employees who are overworked, underpaid, undervalued and you honestly don't want to be there. BUT, you don't know how to get out because you have to work to live.

This **planner** was designed to get you LASER focused on the things you must do daily, weekly, monthly and quarterly in order to build your business so that you are NO longer overworked, underpaid, and undervalued at a JOB! Being laser focused on the bottom line for your business is what will allow you to generate the REVENUE YOU NEED so that you don't have to work a job.

The tools and strategies that I've outlined in this planner are the things I HAD to do in order to be able to **X-it** my job within EIGHT months of seriously building my business. Prior to this, I was trying to do it with no strategy, therefore I got NO results.

I want to stop here and tell you what I DISCOVERED during my journey... it is not our fault that we work at a job. We are conditioned to do that! It's not our fault that all we know to do is work a job all our life, only to realize that when you're too old to work, you still have to work to live because you don't have enough money to live on.

Until we UNLEARN that we must work a job, we will always be stuck being overworked, underpaid and undervalued at a JOB!

I understand, that was me for 33 years, underpaid, undervalued, overworked, etc. I discovered that my 33 year journey in the workforce was not my fault. It's not your fault either that you work a job all your life, it's is a LEARNED behavior!

But, when you know different, you do different. So I'm telling you that working a job is a LEARNED behavior you must work to unlearn. Following the layout of this **planner** is EXACTLY what you need NOW to get started UNLEARNING the behavior of working a job, and LEARNING the behavior of HOW to build the business you have always wanted.

I want to also offer you the opportunity to jump on a call with me to discuss this work cycle you're currently in, and how you can get OUT of it. Whether you've been on your job ONE year or 33 years, if you don't do something NOW, you will always be working at a JOB!

You can schedule a call by going to **bit.ly/xitsession**.

Talk Soon!

Bucket List

The next thing I want you to do is to complete your Bucket List! Take a few moments and ENVISION Your Freedom!

Write down ALL the things you would do. As you are working throughout the year on your FREEDOM, feel free to add more things to the list.

Things I Want To Do

☐ _____

☐ _____

☐ _____

☐ _____

☐ _____

☐ _____

☐ _____

☐ _____

☐ _____

Notes

_____

_____

_____

_____

_____

_____

_____

_____

_____

I promise to stay focused on my dream. Nothing is impossible or unreachable if I just believe. And I believe!

Two things you are in control of in life are your attitude & your effort

Your X-It Date: _____

X-It Goals

20 Things You Will Need To X-It Your Job

GOAL _____   DATE _____

START _____   DEADLINE _____

ACTION STEPS

- You need good time management
- You need to reposition your finances
- You need an idea
- You need a profit plan
- You need a case study
- You need a team and resources
- You need to invest in professional branding
- You need marketing, promotional knowledge, and promotional confidence
- You need support
- You need perseverance
- You need creativity
- You need critical thinking skills
- You need drive and determination
- You need to belief in yourself
- You need to have faith in the Most High
- You need a calculator
- You need patience
- You need expert knowledge or wise counsel
- Surround yourself with like minded people
- You will need a financial plan and focus

BONUS:

You need a BUDGET!

Top 10 Time Thieves

You know that time is one of the most powerful variables you control in your SUCCESS. Now's the time to put a hard stop on your day and live and work better for that clear line in the sand. You already know what some of your biggest time wasters are. But do you know how much total time on these activities your spending and how it affects your REVENUE? Here's a quick exercise to help you decide exactly where a large chunk of your time is being wasted.

How many hours on average do you spend per week doing the following activities?

Minutes/Hours	Event
_____	Performing activities that have no impact on your bottom line revenue.
_____	Doing low-level business activities that you could outsource at a lessor cost than your time.
_____	Making to do lists and not getting things DONE.
_____	Researching instead of investing in business knowledge.
_____	Handling low-value emails, texts or other messages.
_____	Handling low-value requests from people.
_____	Streaming YouTube cat videos, checking social media, or indulging in other forms of escapes.
_____	Putting out fires that could easily have been prevented.
_____	Doing office work/house work you could pay someone to do.
_____	Doing personal errands you could pay someone to do.
_____	**Total: hours per week**

Now that you have identified those things that are **STEALING** your time, it's time to **SHIFT** your thinking to replace those things with **HIGH VALUE** activities that are going to **GROW** your business and generate **REVENUE**.

We are going to work to break the connection between one hour worked and one hour of value created. If on average you can make $75.00 an hour, doesn't it make sense to work and not spend time on things that are not generating **REVENUE**?

PASSWORD TRACKER

WEBSITE	LOGIN	PASSWORD

NOTES

TO DO LIST

YEAR-AT-A-GLANCE

AFFIRMATION: BY THE END OF THIS YEAR, I WILL _____

Yearly Objectives

YEARLY GOAL #1   YEARLY GOAL #2   YEARLY GOAL #3

MISSION   VALUES   FOCUS

Quarterly Objectives

QUARTER 1

1. _____
2. _____
3. _____
4. _____
5. _____

QUARTER 2

1. _____
2. _____
3. _____
4. _____
5. _____

QUARTER 3

1. _____
2. _____
3. _____
4. _____
5. _____

QUARTER 4

1. _____
2. _____
3. _____
4. _____
5. _____

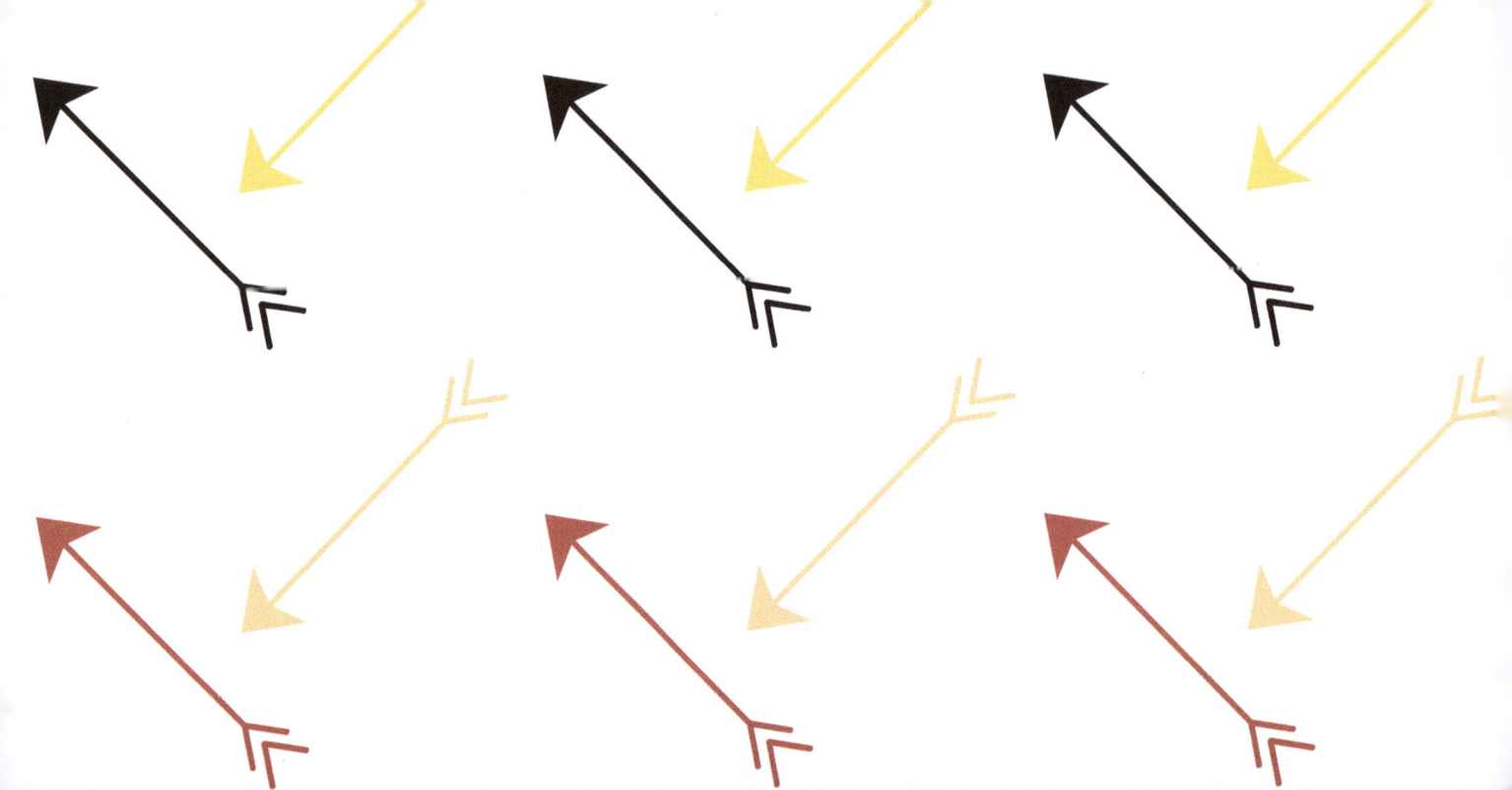

20___

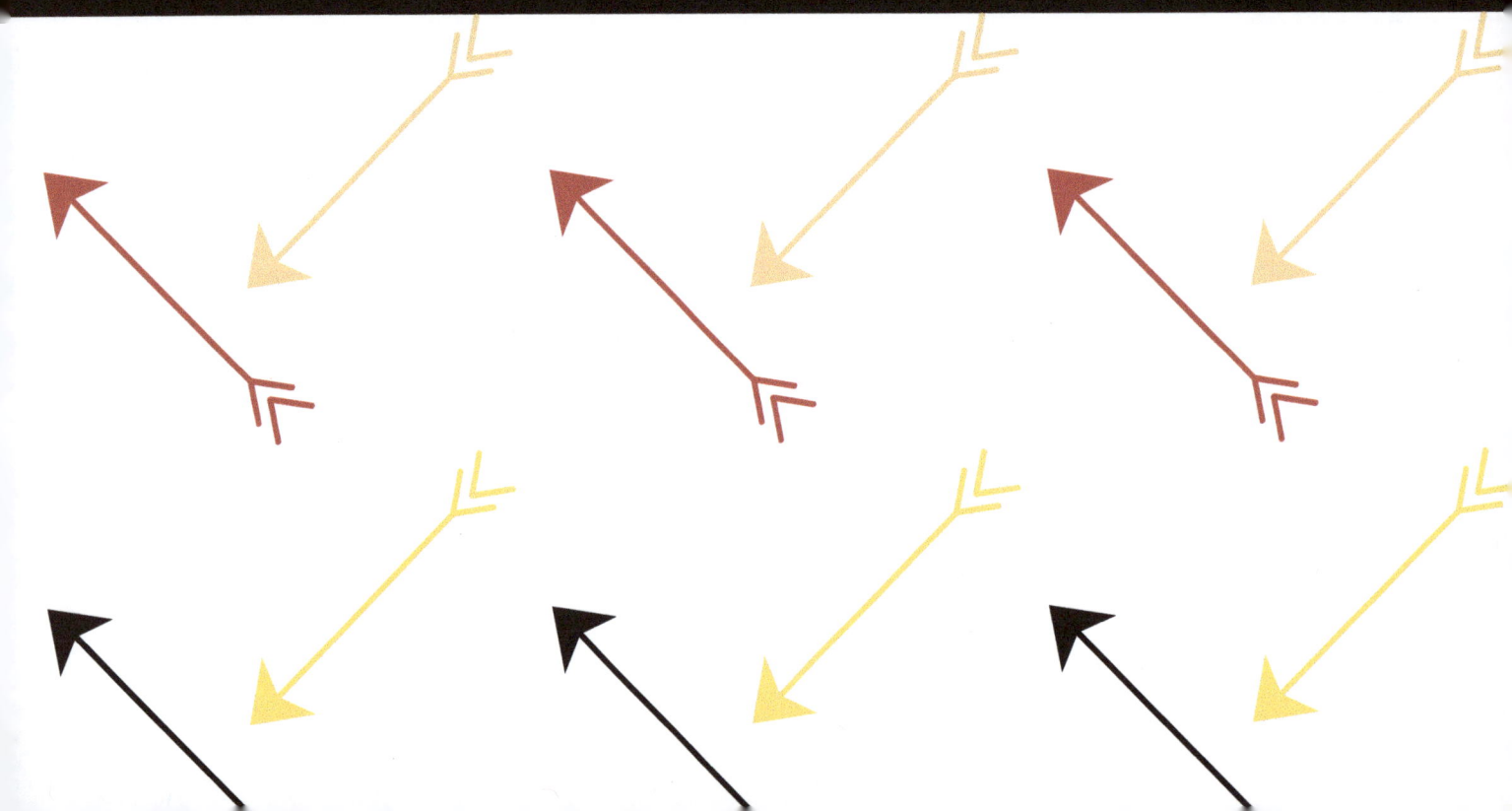

If not now, then when?

JANUARY VISION BOARD

FOCUS OF THE MONTH (PASTE A PICTURE IN THIS SPACE)

Monthly Affirmation

Book Recommendation

20/20 Vision: 20 Things You Need to Quit Your Job in 2020 by Jennifer King

Monthly Budget

Household Expenses (60%)

HOUSING

Mortgage/Rent	$ _____
Home Maintenance	$ _____
Renters' Insurance	$ _____
Utilities (Gas, Water, Electric etc.	$ _____
_____	$ _____

HOUSEHOLD/PERSONAL

Groceries	$ _____
Personal Care	$ _____
Laundry/Dry Clean	$ _____
Professional Dues	$ _____
_____	$ _____
_____	$ _____

CHILDREN

Childcare	$ _____
Education	$ _____
Allowances	$ _____
_____	$ _____
_____	$ _____

HEALTH CARE/INSURANCE

Health Ins.	$ _____
Life Insurance	$ _____
Disability Income Insurance	$ _____
Long Term Care Ins.	$ _____
	$ _____

TRANSPORTATION

Auto Payments	$ _____
Gas	$ _____
Maintenance/ License	$ _____
Parking/Tolls	$ _____
Auto Insurance	$ _____
	$ _____

STUDENT LOANS

Loan 1	$ _____
Loan 2	$ _____
Loan 3	$ _____
Loan 4	$ _____
Subtotal	$ _____

Investing/Saving (20%)

Employees/Contractors	$ _____
Business Courses	$ _____
Technology	$ _____
Retirement Saving (401k, Roth IRA)	$ _____
Regular Savings	$ _____
_____	$ _____

Discretionary Expenses (20%)

Cable/Phone/Internet	$ _____
Dining Out	$ _____
Movies/Events/Hobbies	$ _____
Vacation	$ _____
Gifts/Charity	$ _____
Credit Card Debt Repayment	$ _____
_____	$ _____
_____	$ _____
_____	$ _____

Net Income	$ _____
(Total Expenses)	$ _____
Surplus/(Deficit)	$ _____

Budget Notes

_____
_____
_____
_____
_____

MONTHLY BUSINESS BUDGET

How much does it cost to run your business effectively? Use this worksheet to track business expenses. The more you learn your business and the more you grow, the more you will see the gaps you need to fill in, whether it is technology, staff, office equipment, etc.

TECHNOLOGY	$

STAFF	$

OFFICE EQUIPMENT	$

PROFESSIONAL TRAINING	$

OFFICE SUPPLIES	$

TRAVEL	$

NOTES

January ____

MONDAY	TUESDAY	WEDNESDAY	THURSDAY

The Vision To Quit.

NOTES

Identify
business time
blocks

January Week-at-a-Glance

WEEK 1	WEEK 2	WEEK 3

WEEK 4	WEEK 5	TO DO LIST
		☐ _____
		☐ _____
		☐ _____
		☐ _____

NOTES

January Month-in-Review

REVENUE:

EXPENSES:

REVIEW OF PREVIOUS MONTH REVENUE / EXPENSES

Previous month revenue / expenses:

Where did I have the most trouble?

What could I improve this month?

What Budget Goals can I set for next month?

NEXT MONTH GOALS

RISK ANALYSIS

- [ ]
- [ ]
- [ ]
- [ ]
- [ ]
- [ ]

NOTES

I can do anything I set my mind to.

FEBRUARY VISION BOARD

FOCUS OF THE MONTH (PASTE A PICTURE IN THIS SPACE)

Monthly Affirmation

Book Recommendation

Tribes, We Need You to Lead Us by Seth Godin

Monthly Budget

Household Expenses (60%)

HOUSING

Mortgage/Rent $ _____

Home Maintenance $ _____

Renters' Insurance $ _____

Utilities (Gas, Water, Electric etc. $ _____

_____ $ _____

HOUSEHOLD/PERSONAL

Groceries $ _____

Personal Care $ _____

Laundry/Dry Clean $ _____

Professional Dues $ _____

_____ $ _____

_____ $ _____

CHILDREN

Childcare $ _____

Education $ _____

Allowances $ _____

_____ $ _____

_____ $ _____

HEALTH CARE/INSURANCE

Health Ins. $ _____

Life Insurance $ _____

Disability Income Insurance $ _____

Long Term Care Ins. $ _____

_____ $ _____

TRANSPORTATION

Auto Payments $ _____

Gas $ _____

Maintenance/License $ _____

Parking/Tolls $ _____

Auto Insurance $ _____

_____ $ _____

STUDENT LOANS

Loan 1 $ _____

Loan 2 $ _____

Loan 3 $ _____

Loan 4 $ _____

Subtotal $ _____

Investing/Saving (20%)

Employees/Contractors $ _____

Business Courses $ _____

Technology $ _____

Retirement Saving (401k, Roth IRA) $ _____

Regular Savings $ _____

_____ $ _____

Discretionary Expenses (20%)

Cable/Phone/Internet $ _____

Dining Out $ _____

Movies/Events/Hobbies $ _____

Vacation $ _____

Gifts/Charity $ _____

Credit Card Debt Repayment $ _____

$ _____

$ _____

$ _____

Net Income $ _____

(Total Expenses) $ _____

Surplus/(Deficit) $ _____

Budget Notes

MONTHLY BUSINESS BUDGET

How much does it cost to run your business effectively? Use this worksheet to track business expenses. The more you learn your business and the more you grow, the more you will see the gaps you need to fill in, whether it is technology, staff, office equipment, etc.

TECHNOLOGY	$

STAFF	$

OFFICE EQUIPMENT	$

PROFESSIONAL TRAINING	$

OFFICE SUPPLIES	$

TRAVEL	$

NOTES

February ____

MONDAY	TUESDAY	WEDNESDAY	THURSDAY

For The Love Of Leadership.

FRIDAY	SATURDAY	SUNDAY

Identify business time blocks

February Week-at-a-Glance

WEEK 1	WEEK 2	WEEK 3

WEEK 4	WEEK 5	TO DO LIST
		☐ _____
		☐ _____
		☐ _____
		☐ _____

NOTES

February Month-in-Review

REVIEW OF PREVIOUS MONTH REVENUE / EXPENSES

Previous month revenue / expenses:

Where did I have the most trouble?

What could I improve this month?

What Budget Goals can I set for next month?

NEXT MONTH GOALS

RISK ANALYSIS

☐

☐

☐

☐

☐

☐

NOTES

Follow your heart & your dreams

Your X-It Date: _____

MARCH VISION BOARD

FOCUS OF THE MONTH (PASTE A PICTURE IN THIS SPACE)

Monthly Affirmation

Book Recommendation

The Four Hour Work Week by Tim Ferriss

Monthly Budget

HOUSING

Mortgage/Rent $ _____

Home Maintenance $ _____

Renters' Insurance $ _____

Utilities (Gas, Water, $ _____
Electric etc.

_____ $ _____

HOUSEHOLD/PERSONAL

Groceries $ _____

Personal Care $ _____

Laundry/Dry Clean $ _____

Professional Dues $ _____

_____ $ _____

_____ $ _____

CHILDREN

Childcare $ _____

Education $ _____

Allowances $ _____

_____ $ _____

_____ $ _____

HEALTH CARE/INSURANCE

Health Ins. $ _____

Life Insurance $ _____

Disability Income $ _____
Insurance

Long Term Care $ _____
Ins.

$ _____

TRANSPORTATION

Auto Payments $ _____

Gas $ _____

Maintenance/ $ _____
License

Parking/Tolls $ _____

Auto Insurance $ _____

_____ $ _____

STUDENT LOANS

Loan 1 $ _____

Loan 2 $ _____

Loan 3 $ _____

Loan 4 $ _____

Subtotal $ _____

Employees/Contractors $ _____

Business Courses $ _____

Technology $ _____

Retirement Saving (401k, $ _____
Roth IRA)

Regular Savings $ _____

$ _____

Cable/Phone/Internet $ _____

Dining Out $ _____

Movies/Events/Hobbies $ _____

Vacation $ _____

Gifts/Charity $ _____

Credit Card Debt Repayment $ _____

$ _____

$ _____

$ _____

Net Income $ _____

(Total Expenses $ _____

Surplus/(Deficit $ _____

Budget Notes

MONTHLY BUSINESS BUDGET

How much does it cost to run your business effectively? Use this worksheet to track business expenses. The more you learn your business and the more you grow, the more you will see the gaps you need to fill in, whether it is technology, staff, office equipment, etc.

TECHNOLOGY	$

STAFF	$

OFFICE EQUIPMENT	$

PROFESSIONAL TRAINING	$

OFFICE SUPPLIES	$

TRAVEL	$

NOTES

March ____

MONDAY	TUESDAY	WEDNESDAY	THURSDAY

All Systems Go.

FRIDAY	SATURDAY	SUNDAY

Identify
business time
blocks

March Week-at-a-Glance

WEEK 1	WEEK 2	WEEK 3

WEEK 4	WEEK 5	
		TO DO LIST
		☐ _____
		☐ _____
		☐ _____
		☐ _____

NOTES

_____

_____

_____

_____

March Month-in-Review

REVENUE: | **EXPENSES:**

REVIEW OF PREVIOUS MONTH REVENUE / EXPENSES

Previous month revenue / expenses:

Where did I have the most trouble?

What could I improve this month?

What Budget Goals can I set for next month?

NEXT MONTH GOALS

RISK ANALYSIS

☐

☐

☐

☐

☐

☐

NOTES

QUARTERLY BUSINESS SOOT ANALYSIS

A S-O-O-T Analysis is a structured way to see where your business stands today relative to it's top goal. This tool helps you lay out the key landmarks from which to plan your strategy so that you can get FREE!

STRENGTHS

Any strategy you choose must rely on your strengths while keeping your goal of FREEDOM in Mind! Keeping this goal in mind, what are your top FIVE strengths you can draw on to accomplish this goal?

☐ _____

☐ _____

☐ _____

☐ _____

☐ _____

OBSTACLES

Each key obstacle is a clue as to what next steps you need to take in your business. What are the FIVE biggest obstacles that is blocking you from achieving your FREEDOM?

☐ _____

☐ _____

☐ _____

☐ _____

☐ _____

OPPORTUNITIES

Opportunities are where you win the game in business. What are the THREE biggest opportunities you can pursue that potentially could help achieve your FREEDOM?

☐ _____

☐ _____

☐ _____

THREATS

What are the THREE biggest threats that could literally put you out of business? The goal is to take simple proactive steps now to mitigate dangers later.

☐ _____

☐ _____

☐ _____

When things change inside you, things change around you

APRIL VISION BOARD

FOCUS OF THE MONTH (PASTE A PICTURE IN THIS SPACE)

Monthly Affirmation

Book Recommendation

Relentless by Tim Grover

Monthly Budget

Household Expenses (60%)

HOUSING

Mortgage/Rent $ _____

Home Maintenance $ _____

Renters' Insurance $ _____

Utilities (Gas, Water, $ _____
Electric etc.

_____ $ _____

HOUSEHOLD/PERSONAL

Groceries $ _____

Personal Care $ _____

Laundry/Dry Clean $ _____

Professional Dues $ _____

_____ $ _____

_____ $ _____

CHILDREN

Childcare $ _____

Education $ _____

Allowances $ _____

_____ $ _____

_____ $ _____

HEALTH CARE/INSURANCE

Health Ins. $ _____

Life Insurance $ _____

Disability Income $ _____
Insurance

Long Term Care $ _____
Ins.

_____ $ _____

TRANSPORTATION

Auto Payments $ _____

Gas $ _____

Maintenance/ $ _____
License

Parking/Tolls $ _____

Auto Insurance $ _____

_____ $ _____

STUDENT LOANS

Loan 1 $ _____

Loan 2 $ _____

Loan 3 $ _____

Loan 4 $ _____

Subtotal $ _____

Investing/Saving (20%)

Employees/Contractors $ _____

Business Courses $ _____

Technology $ _____

Retirement Saving (401k, $ _____
Roth IRA)

Regular Savings $ _____

_____ $ _____

Discretionary Expenses (20%)

Cable/Phone/Internet $ _____

Dining Out $ _____

Movies/Events/Hobbies $ _____

Vacation $ _____

Gifts/Charity $ _____

Credit Card Debt Repayment $ _____

_____ $ _____

_____ $ _____

_____ $ _____

Net Income $ _____

(Total Expenses) $ _____

Surplus/(Deficit) $ _____

Budget Notes

MONTHLY BUSINESS BUDGET

How much does it cost to run your business effectively? Use this worksheet to track business expenses. The more you learn your business and the more you grow, the more you will see the gaps you need to fill in, whether it is technology, staff, office equipment, etc.

TECHNOLOGY	$

STAFF	$

OFFICE EQUIPMENT	$

PROFESSIONAL TRAINING	$

OFFICE SUPPLIES	$

TRAVEL	$

NOTES

April ____

MONDAY	TUESDAY	WEDNESDAY	THURSDAY

Don't Be No Fool.

FRIDAY	SATURDAY	SUNDAY

NOTES

Identify
business time
blocks

April Week-at-a-Glance

WEEK 1	WEEK 2	WEEK 3

WEEK 4	WEEK 5	

TO DO LIST

☐ _____

☐ _____

☐ _____

☐ _____

NOTES

April Month-in-Review

REVENUE:

EXPENSES:

REVIEW OF PREVIOUS MONTH REVENUE / EXPENSES

Previous month revenue / expenses:

Where did I have the most trouble?

What could I improve this month?

What Budget Goals can I set for next month?

NEXT MONTH GOALS

RISK ANALYSIS

- [ ]
- [ ]
- [ ]
- [ ]
- [ ]
- [ ]

NOTES

You are enough

Your X-It Date: _____

MAY VISION BOARD

FOCUS OF THE MONTH (PASTE A PICTURE IN THIS SPACE)

Monthly Affirmation

Book Recommendation

33 Years a Slave: Removing Chains from Life, Love and Business and Companion Journal by Jennifer King

Monthly Budget

Household Expenses (60%)

HOUSING

Mortgage/Rent $ _____

Home Maintenance $ _____

Renters' Insurance $ _____

Utilities (Gas, Water, Electric etc. $ _____

_____ $ _____

HOUSEHOLD/PERSONAL

Groceries $ _____

Personal Care $ _____

Laundry/Dry Clean $ _____

Professional Dues $ _____

_____ $ _____

_____ $ _____

CHILDREN

Childcare $ _____

Education $ _____

Allowances $ _____

_____ $ _____

_____ $ _____

HEALTH CARE/INSURANCE

Health Ins. $ _____

Life Insurance $ _____

Disability Income Insurance $ _____

Long Term Care Ins. $ _____

_____ $ _____

TRANSPORTATION

Auto Payments $ _____

Gas $ _____

Maintenance/License $ _____

Parking/Tolls $ _____

Auto Insurance $ _____

_____ $ _____

STUDENT LOANS

Loan 1 $ _____

Loan 2 $ _____

Loan 3 $ _____

Loan 4 $ _____

Subtotal $ _____

Investing/Saving (20%)

Employees/Contractors $ _____

Business Courses $ _____

Technology $ _____

Retirement Saving (401k, Roth IRA) $ _____

Regular Savings $ _____

_____ $ _____

Discretionary Expenses (20%)

Cable/Phone/Internet $ _____

Dining Out $ _____

Movies/Events/Hobbies $ _____

Vacation $ _____

Gifts/Charity $ _____

Credit Card Debt Repayment $ _____

_____ $ _____

_____ $ _____

_____ $ _____

Net Income $ _____

(Total Expenses) $ _____

Surplus/(Deficit) $ _____

Budget Notes

MONTHLY BUSINESS BUDGET

How much does it cost to run your business effectively? Use this worksheet to track business expenses. The more you learn your business and the more you grow, the more you will see the gaps you need to fill in, whether it is technology, staff, office equipment, etc.

TECHNOLOGY	$

STAFF	$

OFFICE EQUIPMENT	$

PROFESSIONAL TRAINING	$

OFFICE SUPPLIES	$

TRAVEL	$

NOTES

May ____

MONDAY	TUESDAY	WEDNESDAY	THURSDAY

MAYke It Happen.

Identify
business time
blocks

May Week-at-a-Glance

WEEK 1	WEEK 2	WEEK 3

WEEK 4	WEEK 5	
		TO DO LIST

TO DO LIST

- ☐ _____
- ☐ _____
- ☐ _____
- ☐ _____

NOTES

_____
_____
_____
_____

May Month-in-Review

REVENUE:

EXPENSES:

REVIEW OF PREVIOUS MONTH REVENUE / EXPENSES

Previous month revenue / expenses:

Where did I have the most trouble?

What could I improve this month?

What Budget Goals can I set for next month?

NEXT MONTH GOALS

RISK ANALYSIS

- [ ]
- [ ]
- [ ]
- [ ]
- [ ]
- [ ]

NOTES

You are necessary!

Your X-It Date: _____

JUNE VISION BOARD

Monthly Affirmation

Book Recommendation

Passion, Purpose & Profit: Shifting Your Dreams into Successful Entrepreneurship by Dawniel Winningham

Monthly Budget

HOUSING

Mortgage/Rent $ _____

Home Maintenance $ _____

Renters' Insurance $ _____

Utilities (Gas, Water, $ _____
Electric etc.

_____ $ _____

HOUSEHOLD/PERSONAL

Groceries $ _____

Personal Care $ _____

Laundry/Dry Clean $ _____

Professional Dues $ _____

_____ $ _____

_____ $ _____

CHILDREN

Childcare $ _____

Education $ _____

Allowances $ _____

_____ $ _____

_____ $ _____

HEALTH CARE/INSURANCE

Health Ins. $ _____

Life Insurance $ _____

Disability Income $ _____
Insurance

Long Term Care $ _____
Ins.

$ _____

TRANSPORTATION

Auto Payments $ _____

Gas $ _____

Maintenance/ $ _____
License

Parking/Tolls $ _____

Auto Insurance $ _____

_____ $ _____

STUDENT LOANS

Loan 1 $ _____

Loan 2 $ _____

Loan 3 $ _____

Loan 4 $ _____

Subtotal $ _____

Investing/Saving (20%)

Employees/Contractors $ _____

Business Courses $ _____

Technology $ _____

Retirement Saving (401k, $ _____
Roth IRA)

Regular Savings $ _____

_____ $ _____

Discretionary Expenses (20%)

Cable/Phone/Internet $ _____

Dining Out $ _____

Movies/Events/Hobbies $ _____

Vacation $ _____

Gifts/Charity $ _____

Credit Card Debt Repayment $ _____

_____ $ _____

_____ $ _____

_____ $ _____

Net Income $ _____

(Total Expenses) $ _____

Surplus/(Deficit) $ _____

Budget Notes

_____

_____

_____

_____

_____

_____

MONTHLY BUSINESS BUDGET

How much does it cost to run your business effectively? Use this worksheet to track business expenses. The more you learn your business and the more you grow, the more you will see the gaps you need to fill in, whether it is technology, staff, office equipment, etc.

TECHNOLOGY	$

STAFF	$

OFFICE EQUIPMENT	$

PROFESSIONAL TRAINING	$

OFFICE SUPPLIES	$

TRAVEL	$

NOTES

June ____

MONDAY	TUESDAY	WEDNESDAY	THURSDAY

Heat Up Your Business.

FRIDAY	SATURDAY	SUNDAY	
			Identify business time blocks

June Week-at-a-Glance

WEEK 1	WEEK 2	WEEK 3

WEEK 4	WEEK 5	
		TO DO LIST

TO DO LIST

- ☐ _____
- ☐ _____
- ☐ _____
- ☐ _____

NOTES

June Month-in-Review

REVENUE:

EXPENSES:

REVIEW OF PREVIOUS MONTH REVENUE / EXPENSES

Previous month revenue / expenses:

Where did I have the most trouble?

What could I improve this month?

What Budget Goals can I set for next month?

NEXT MONTH GOALS

RISK ANALYSIS

☐

☐

☐

☐

☐

☐

NOTES

QUARTERLY BUSINESS SOOT ANALYSIS

A S-O-O-T Analysis is a structured way to see where your business stands today relative to it's top goal. This tool helps you lay out the key landmarks from which to plan your strategy so that you can get FREE!

STRENGTHS

Any strategy you choose must rely on your strengths while keeping your goal of FREEDOM in Mind! Keeping this goal in mind, what are your top FIVE strengths you can draw on to accomplish this goal?

☐ _____

☐ _____

☐ _____

☐ _____

☐ _____

OBSTACLES

Each key obstacle is a clue as to what next steps you need to take in your business. What are the FIVE biggest obstacles that is blocking you from achieving your FREEDOM?

☐ _____

☐ _____

☐ _____

☐ _____

☐ _____

OPPORTUNITIES

Opportunities are where you win the game in business. What are the THREE biggest opportunities you can pursue that potentially could help achieve your FREEDOM?

☐ _____

☐ _____

☐ _____

THREATS

What are the THREE biggest threats that could literally put you out of business? The goal is to take simple proactive steps now to mitigate dangers later.

☐ _____

☐ _____

☐ _____

Doubt kills more dreams than failure ever will

Your X-It Date: _____

JULY VISION BOARD

Monthly Affirmation

Book Recommendation

How to Win Friends and Influence People by Dale Carnegie

Monthly Budget

Household Expenses (60%)

HOUSING

Mortgage/Rent $ _____

Home Maintenance $ _____

Renters' Insurance $ _____

Utilities (Gas, Water, Electric etc. $ _____

_____ $ _____

HOUSEHOLD/PERSONAL

Groceries $ _____

Personal Care $ _____

Laundry/Dry Clean $ _____

Professional Dues $ _____

_____ $ _____

_____ $ _____

CHILDREN

Childcare $ _____

Education $ _____

Allowances $ _____

_____ $ _____

_____ $ _____

HEALTH CARE/INSURANCE

Health Ins. $ _____

Life Insurance $ _____

Disability Income Insurance $ _____

Long Term Care Ins. $ _____

_____ $ _____

TRANSPORTATION

Auto Payments $ _____

Gas $ _____

Maintenance/ License $ _____

Parking/Tolls $ _____

Auto Insurance $ _____

_____ $ _____

STUDENT LOANS

Loan 1 $ _____

Loan 2 $ _____

Loan 3 $ _____

Loan 4 $ _____

Subtotal $ _____

Investing/Saving (20%)

Employees/Contractors $ _____

Business Courses $ _____

Technology $ _____

Retirement Saving (401k, Roth IRA) $ _____

Regular Savings $ _____

_____ $ _____

Discretionary Expenses (20%)

Cable/Phone/Internet $ _____

Dining Out $ _____

Movies/Events/Hobbies $ _____

Vacation $ _____

Gifts/Charity $ _____

Credit Card Debt Repayment $ _____

_____ $ _____

_____ $ _____

_____ $ _____

Net Income $ _____

(Total Expenses) $ _____

Surplus/(Deficit) $ _____

Budget Notes

MONTHLY BUSINESS BUDGET

How much does it cost to run your business effectively? Use this worksheet to track business expenses. The more you learn your business and the more you grow, the more you will see the gaps you need to fill in, whether it is technology, staff, office equipment, etc.

TECHNOLOGY	$

STAFF	$

OFFICE EQUIPMENT	$

PROFESSIONAL TRAINING	$

OFFICE SUPPLIES	$

TRAVEL	$

NOTES

July ____

MONDAY	TUESDAY	WEDNESDAY	THURSDAY

Red, White and Blue and Read, Work and Build.

FRIDAY	SATURDAY	SUNDAY

Identify business time blocks

July Week-at-a-Glance

WEEK 1	WEEK 2	WEEK 3

WEEK 4	WEEK 5	TO DO LIST
		☐ _____
		☐ _____
		☐ _____
		☐ _____

NOTES

July Month-in-Review

REVENUE: **EXPENSES:**

REVIEW OF PREVIOUS MONTH REVENUE / EXPENSES

Previous month revenue / expenses:

Where did I have the most trouble?

What could I improve this month?

What Budget Goals can I set for next month?

NEXT MONTH GOALS   **RISK ANALYSIS**

- [ ]
- [ ]
- [ ]
- [ ]
- [ ]
- [ ]

NOTES

What is coming is better than what is gone

Your X-It Date: _____

AUGUST VISION BOARD

FOCUS OF THE MONTH (PASTE A PICTURE IN THIS SPACE)

Monthly Affirmation

Book Recommendation

Select an industry specific book to read

Monthly Budget

HOUSING

Mortgage/Rent $ _____

Home Maintenance $ _____

Renters' Insurance $ _____

Utilities (Gas, Water, Electric etc. $ _____

_____ $ _____

HOUSEHOLD/PERSONAL

Groceries $ _____

Personal Care $ _____

Laundry/Dry Clean $ _____

Professional Dues $ _____

_____ $ _____

_____ $ _____

CHILDREN

Childcare $ _____

Education $ _____

Allowances $ _____

_____ $ _____

_____ $ _____

HEALTH CARE/INSURANCE

Health Ins. $ _____

Life Insurance $ _____

Disability Income Insurance $ _____

Long Term Care Ins. $ _____

_____ $ _____

TRANSPORTATION

Auto Payments $ _____

Gas $ _____

Maintenance/ License $ _____

Parking/Tolls $ _____

Auto Insurance $ _____

_____ $ _____

STUDENT LOANS

Loan 1 $ _____

Loan 2 $ _____

Loan 3 $ _____

Loan 4 $ _____

Subtotal $ _____

Investing/Saving (20%)

Employees/Contractors $ _____

Business Courses $ _____

Technology $ _____

Retirement Saving (401k, Roth IRA) $ _____

Regular Savings $ _____

_____ $ _____

Discretionary Expenses (20%)

Cable/Phone/Internet $ _____

Dining Out $ _____

Movies/Events/Hobbies $ _____

Vacation $ _____

Gifts/Charity $ _____

Credit Card Debt Repayment $ _____

_____ $ _____

_____ $ _____

_____ $ _____

_____ $ _____

Net Income $ _____

(Total Expenses) $ _____

Surplus/(Deficit) $ _____

Budget Notes

MONTHLY BUSINESS BUDGET

How much does it cost to run your business effectively? Use this worksheet to track business expenses. The more you learn your business and the more you grow, the more you will see the gaps you need to fill in, whether it is technology, staff, office equipment, etc.

TECHNOLOGY	$

STAFF	$

OFFICE EQUIPMENT	$

PROFESSIONAL TRAINING	$

OFFICE SUPPLIES	$

TRAVEL	$

NOTES

August ____

MONDAY	TUESDAY	WEDNESDAY	THURSDAY

Back To School.

FRIDAY	SATURDAY	SUNDAY

NOTES

Identify business time blocks

August Week-at-a-Glance

WEEK 1	WEEK 2	WEEK 3

WEEK 4	WEEK 5	TO DO LIST
		☐ _____
		☐ _____
		☐ _____
		☐ _____

NOTES

_____

_____

_____

_____

August Month-in-Review

REVENUE:

EXPENSES:

REVIEW OF PREVIOUS MONTH REVENUE / EXPENSES

Previous month revenue / expenses:

Where did I have the most trouble?

What could I improve this month?

What Budget Goals can I set for next month?

NEXT MONTH GOALS

RISK ANALYSIS

- [ ]
- [ ]
- [ ]
- [ ]
- [ ]
- [ ]

NOTES

Be bold, be fearless

Your X-It Date: _____

SEPTEMBER VISION BOARD

FOCUS OF THE MONTH (PASTE A PICTURE IN THIS SPACE)

Monthly Affirmation

Book Recommendation

Poke the Box by Seth Godin

Monthly Budget

Household Expenses (60%)

HOUSING

Mortgage/Rent $ _____

Home Maintenance $ _____

Renters' Insurance $ _____

Utilities (Gas, Water, Electric etc. $ _____

_____ $ _____

HOUSEHOLD/PERSONAL

Groceries $ _____

Personal Care $ _____

Laundry/Dry Clean $ _____

Professional Dues $ _____

_____ $ _____

_____ $ _____

CHILDREN

Childcare $ _____

Education $ _____

Allowances $ _____

_____ $ _____

_____ $ _____

HEALTH CARE/INSURANCE

Health Ins. $ _____

Life Insurance $ _____

Disability Income Insurance $ _____

Long Term Care Ins. $ _____

_____ $ _____

TRANSPORTATION

Auto Payments $ _____

Gas $ _____

Maintenance/ License $ _____

Parking/Tolls $ _____

Auto Insurance $ _____

_____ $ _____

STUDENT LOANS

Loan 1 $ _____

Loan 2 $ _____

Loan 3 $ _____

Loan 4 $ _____

Subtotal $ _____

Investing/Saving (20%)

Employees/Contractors $ _____

Business Courses $ _____

Technology $ _____

Retirement Saving (401k, Roth IRA) $ _____

Regular Savings $ _____

_____ $ _____

Discretionary Expenses (20%)

Cable/Phone/Internet $ _____

Dining Out $ _____

Movies/Events/Hobbies $ _____

Vacation $ _____

Gifts/Charity $ _____

Credit Card Debt Repayment $ _____

_____ $ _____

_____ $ _____

_____ $ _____

Net Income $ _____

(Total Expenses) $ _____

Surplus/(Deficit) $ _____

Budget Notes

MONTHLY BUSINESS BUDGET

How much does it cost to run your business effectively? Use this worksheet to track business expenses. The more you learn your business and the more you grow, the more you will see the gaps you need to fill in, whether it is technology, staff, office equipment, etc.

TECHNOLOGY	$

STAFF	$

PROFESSIONAL TRAINING	$

OFFICE EQUIPMENT	$

OFFICE SUPPLIES	$

TRAVEL	$

NOTES

September ____

MONDAY	TUESDAY	WEDNESDAY	THURSDAY

Labor In YOUR Business.

FRIDAY	SATURDAY	SUNDAY

September Week-at-a-Glance

WEEK 1	WEEK 2	WEEK 3

WEEK 4	WEEK 5	TO DO LIST
		☐ _____
		☐ _____
		☐ _____
		☐ _____

NOTES

September Month-in-Review

REVENUE:

EXPENSES:

REVIEW OF PREVIOUS MONTH REVENUE / EXPENSES

Previous month revenue / expenses:

Where did I have the most trouble?

What could I improve this month?

What Budget Goals can I set for next month?

NEXT MONTH GOALS

RISK ANALYSIS

- [ ]
- [ ]
- [ ]
- [ ]
- [ ]
- [ ]

NOTES

QUARTERLY BUSINESS SOOT ANALYSIS

A S-O-O-T Analysis is a structured way to see where your business stands today relative to it's top goal. This tool helps you lay out the key landmarks from which to plan your strategy so that you can get FREE!

STRENGTHS

Any strategy you choose must rely on your strengths while keeping your goal of FREEDOM in Mind! Keeping this goal in mind, what are your top FIVE strengths you can draw on to accomplish this goal?

- ☐ _____
- ☐ _____
- ☐ _____
- ☐ _____
- ☐ _____

OBSTACLES

Each key obstacle is a clue as to what next steps you need to take in your business. What are the FIVE biggest obstacles that is blocking you from achieving your FREEDOM?

- ☐ _____
- ☐ _____
- ☐ _____
- ☐ _____
- ☐ _____

OPPORTUNITIES

Opportunities are where you win the game in business. What are the THREE biggest opportunities you can pursue that potentially could help achieve your FREEDOM?

- ☐ _____
- ☐ _____
- ☐ _____

THREATS

What are the THREE biggest threats that could literally put you out of business? The goal is to take simple proactive steps now to mitigate dangers later.

- ☐ _____
- ☐ _____
- ☐ _____

Your next chapter is going to be amazing

Your X-It Date: _____

OCTOBER VISION BOARD

FOCUS OF THE MONTH (PASTE A PICTURE IN THIS SPACE)

Monthly Affirmation

Book Recommendation

The 10X Rule by Grant Cardone

Monthly Budget

HOUSING

Mortgage/Rent $_____

Home Maintenance $_____

Renters' Insurance $_____

Utilities (Gas, Water, $_____
Electric etc.

_____ $_____

HOUSEHOLD/PERSONAL

Groceries $_____

Personal Care $_____

Laundry/Dry Clean $_____

Professional Dues $_____

_____ $_____

_____ $_____

CHILDREN

Childcare $_____

Education $_____

Allowances $_____

_____ $_____

_____ $_____

HEALTH CARE/INSURANCE

Health Ins. $_____

Life Insurance $_____

Disability Income $_____
Insurance

Long Term Care $_____
Ins.

_____ $_____

TRANSPORTATION

Auto Payments $_____

Gas $_____

Maintenance/ $_____
License

Parking/Tolls $_____

Auto Insurance $_____

_____ $_____

STUDENT LOANS

Loan 1 $_____

Loan 2 $_____

Loan 3 $_____

Loan 4 $_____

Subtotal $_____

Investing/Saving (20%)

Employees/Contractors $_____

Business Courses $_____

Technology $_____

Retirement Saving (401k, $_____
Roth IRA)

Regular Savings $_____

_____ $_____

Discretionary Expenses (20%)

Cable/Phone/Internet $_____

Dining Out $_____

Movies/Events/Hobbies $_____

Vacation $_____

Gifts/Charity $_____

Credit Card Debt Repayment $_____

_____ $_____

_____ $_____

_____ $_____

Net Income $_____

(Total Expenses) $_____

Surplus/(Deficit) $_____

Budget Notes

MONTHLY BUSINESS BUDGET

How much does it cost to run your business effectively? Use this worksheet to track business expenses. The more you learn your business and the more you grow, the more you will see the gaps you need to fill in, whether it is technology, staff, office equipment, etc.

TECHNOLOGY	$

STAFF	$

OFFICE EQUIPMENT	$

PROFESSIONAL TRAINING	$

OFFICE SUPPLIES	$

TRAVEL	$

NOTES

October ____

MONDAY	TUESDAY	WEDNESDAY	THURSDAY

Fall Finances.

FRIDAY	SATURDAY	SUNDAY

Identify business time blocks

October Week-at-a-Glance

WEEK 1	WEEK 2	WEEK 3

WEEK 4	WEEK 5

TO DO LIST

☐ _____

☐ _____

☐ _____

☐ _____

NOTES

_____

_____

_____

_____

October Month-in-Review

REVENUE:

EXPENSES:

REVIEW OF PREVIOUS MONTH REVENUE / EXPENSES

Previous month revenue / expenses:

Where did I have the most trouble?

What could I improve this month?

What Budget Goals can I set for next month?

NEXT MONTH GOALS

RISK ANALYSIS

- [ ]
- [ ]
- [ ]
- [ ]
- [ ]
- [ ]

NOTES

Do it afraid,

as long as

you do it

NOVEMBER VISION BOARD

Monthly Affirmation

Book Recommendation

Go Live and Get Green: 20+ Ways Entrepreneurs are Using LiveStream to Create More Connections and More Cash by Dawniel Winningham

Monthly Budget

HOUSING

Mortgage/Rent $_____

Home Maintenance $_____

Renters' Insurance $_____

Utilities (Gas, Water, $_____
Electric etc.

_____ $_____

HOUSEHOLD/PERSONAL

Groceries $_____

Personal Care $_____

Laundry/Dry Clean $_____

Professional Dues $_____

_____ $_____

_____ $_____

CHILDREN

Childcare $_____

Education $_____

Allowances $_____

_____ $_____

_____ $_____

HEALTH CARE/INSURANCE

Health Ins. $_____

Life Insurance $_____

Disability Income $_____
Insurance

Long Term Care $_____
Ins.

_____ $_____

TRANSPORTATION

Auto Payments $_____

Gas $_____

Maintenance/ $_____
License

Parking/Tolls $_____

Auto Insurance $_____

_____ $_____

STUDENT LOANS

Loan 1 $_____

Loan 2 $_____

Loan 3 $_____

Loan 4 $_____

Subtotal $_____

Investing/Saving (20%)

Employees/Contractors $_____

Business Courses $_____

Technology $_____

Retirement Saving (401k, $_____
Roth IRA)

Regular Savings $_____

_____ $_____

Discretionary Expenses (20%)

Cable/Phone/Internet $_____

Dining Out $_____

Movies/Events/Hobbies $_____

Vacation $_____

Gifts/Charity $_____

Credit Card Debt Repayment $_____

_____ $_____

_____ $_____

_____ $_____

Net Income $_____

(Total Expenses) $_____

Surplus/(Deficit) $_____

Budget Notes

MONTHLY BUSINESS BUDGET

How much does it cost to run your business effectively? Use this worksheet to track business expenses. The more you learn your business and the more you grow, the more you will see the gaps you need to fill in, whether it is technology, staff, office equipment, etc.

TECHNOLOGY	$

STAFF	$

OFFICE EQUIPMENT	$

PROFESSIONAL TRAINING	$

OFFICE SUPPLIES	$

TRAVEL	$

NOTES

November ____

MONDAY	TUESDAY	WEDNESDAY	THURSDAY

MONDAY	TUESDAY	WEDNESDAY	THURSDAY

Never Stop Promoting.

FRIDAY	SATURDAY	SUNDAY

Identify
business time
blocks

November Week-at-a-Glance

WEEK 1	WEEK 2	WEEK 3

WEEK 4	WEEK 5	

TO DO LIST

- [ ] _____
- [ ] _____
- [ ] _____
- [ ] _____

NOTES

_____

_____

_____

_____

November Month-in-Review

REVIEW OF PREVIOUS MONTH REVENUE / EXPENSES

Previous month revenue / expenses:

Where did I have the most trouble?

What could I improve this month?

What Budget Goals can I set for next month?

NEXT MONTH GOALS

RISK ANALYSIS

- [ ]
- [ ]
- [ ]
- [ ]
- [ ]
- [ ]

NOTES

There are people who need your help & they are waiting for you to show up...

Your X-It Date: _____

DECEMBER VISION BOARD

FOCUS OF THE MONTH (PASTE A PICTURE IN THIS SPACE)

Monthly Affirmation

Book Recommendation

Creating Killer Social Media Content
Workbook by Jennifer King

Monthly Budget

Household Expenses (60%)

HOUSING

Mortgage/Rent $_____

Home Maintenance $_____

Renters' Insurance $_____

Utilities (Gas, Water, Electric etc. $_____

_____ $_____

HOUSEHOLD/PERSONAL

Groceries $_____

Personal Care $_____

Laundry/Dry Clean $_____

Professional Dues $_____

_____ $_____

_____ $_____

CHILDREN

Childcare $_____

Education $_____

Allowances $_____

_____ $_____

_____ $_____

HEALTH CARE/INSURANCE

Health Ins. $_____

Life Insurance $_____

Disability Income Insurance $_____

Long Term Care Ins. $_____

_____ $_____

TRANSPORTATION

Auto Payments $_____

Gas $_____

Maintenance/License $_____

Parking/Tolls $_____

Auto Insurance $_____

_____ $_____

STUDENT LOANS

Loan 1 $_____

Loan 2 $_____

Loan 3 $_____

Loan 4 $_____

Subtotal $_____

Investing/Saving (20%)

Employees/Contractors $_____

Business Courses $_____

Technology $_____

Retirement Saving (401k, Roth IRA) $_____

Regular Savings $_____

_____ $_____

Discretionary Expenses (20%)

Cable/Phone/Internet $_____

Dining Out $_____

Movies/Events/Hobbies $_____

Vacation $_____

Gifts/Charity $_____

Credit Card Debt Repayment $_____

_____ $_____

_____ $_____

_____ $_____

Net Income $_____

(Total Expenses) $_____

Surplus/(Deficit) $_____

Budget Notes

MONTHLY BUSINESS BUDGET

How much does it cost to run your business effectively? Use this worksheet to track business expenses. The more you learn your business and the more you grow, the more you will see the gaps you need to fill in, whether it is technology, staff, office equipment, etc.

TECHNOLOGY	$

STAFF	$

OFFICE EQUIPMENT	$

PROFESSIONAL TRAINING	$

OFFICE SUPPLIES	$

TRAVEL	$

NOTES

December ____

MONDAY	TUESDAY	WEDNESDAY	THURSDAY

Content Creation.

FRIDAY	SATURDAY	SUNDAY

Identify
business time
blocks

December Week-at-a-Glance

WEEK 1	WEEK 2	WEEK 3

WEEK 4	WEEK 5	

TO DO LIST

- [ ] _____
- [ ] _____
- [ ] _____
- [ ] _____

NOTES

December Month-in-Review

REVENUE:

EXPENSES:

REVIEW OF PREVIOUS MONTH REVENUE / EXPENSES

Previous month revenue / expenses:

Where did I have the most trouble?

What could I improve this month?

What Budget Goals can I set for next month?

NEXT MONTH GOALS

RISK ANALYSIS

- [ ]
- [ ]
- [ ]
- [ ]
- [ ]
- [ ]

NOTES

QUARTERLY BUSINESS SOOT ANALYSIS

A S-O-O-T Analysis is a structured way to see where your business stands today relative to it's top goal. This tool helps you lay out the key landmarks from which to plan your strategy so that you can get FREE!

STRENGTHS

Any strategy you choose must rely on your strengths while keeping your goal of FREEDOM in Mind! Keeping this goal in mind, what are your top FIVE strengths you can draw on to accomplish this goal?

☐ _____

☐ _____

☐ _____

☐ _____

☐ _____

OBSTACLES

Each key obstacle is a clue as to what next steps you need to take in your business. What are the FIVE biggest obstacles that is blocking you from achieving your FREEDOM?

☐ _____

☐ _____

☐ _____

☐ _____

☐ _____

OPPORTUNITIES

Opportunities are where you win the game in business. What are the THREE biggest opportunities you can pursue that potentially could help achieve your FREEDOM?

☐ _____

☐ _____

☐ _____

THREATS

What are the THREE biggest threats that could literally put you out of business? The goal is to take simple proactive steps now to mitigate dangers later.

☐ _____

☐ _____

☐ _____

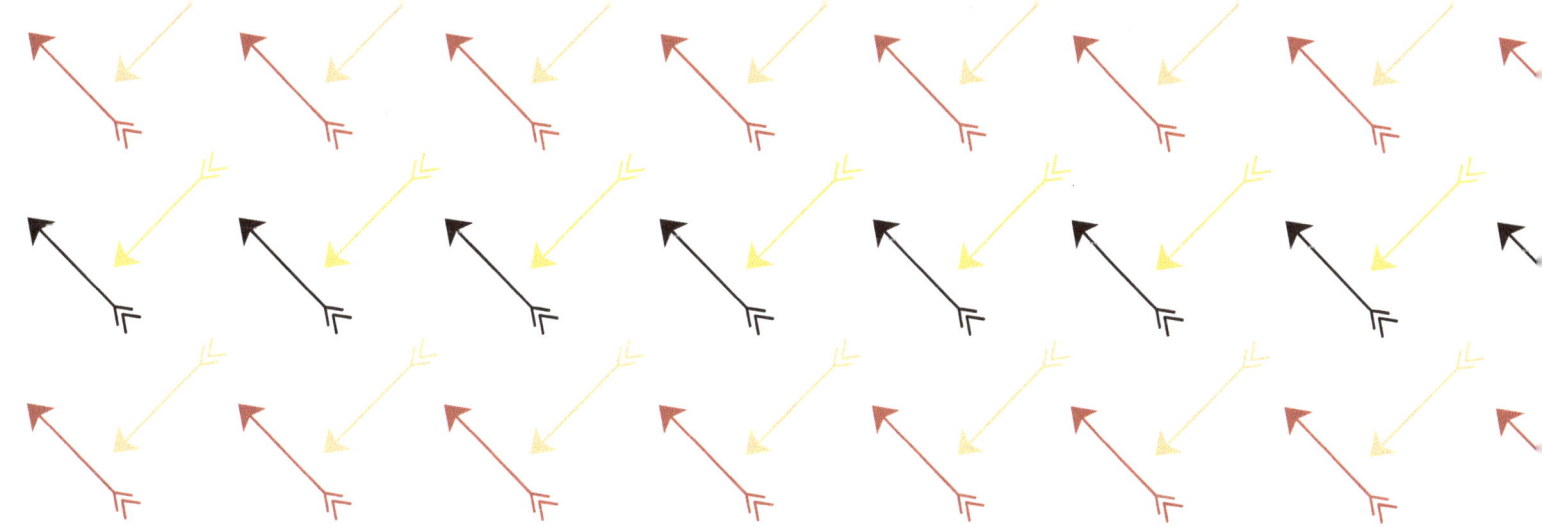

Sample

RESIGNATION
Letter

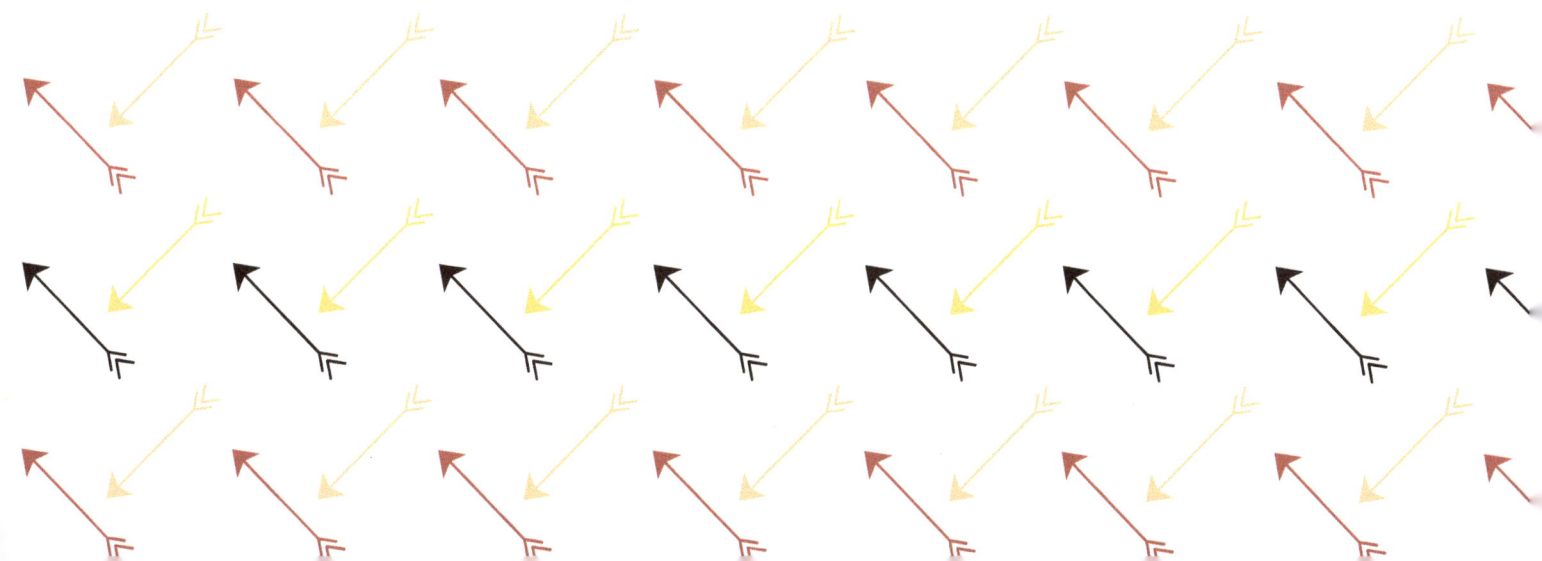

Your Name
Your Street Address
Your City, State & Zip Code
Your Phone Number
Your Email Address

[Date]

Supervisor/Manager Name
Title
Company Name
Company Street Address
Company City, State & Zip Code

Dear [Supervisor/Manager Name],

Please accept this letter as notice of my resignation from my position as [position]. My last day of employment will be [date].

I appreciate the opportunities I have been given during my time with your company, as well as your professional guidance and support. I wish you and the company the best of success in the future.

If I can assist with the transition to my successor, please do let me know.

Very sincerely,

Signature (hard copy letter)

NOTES

NOTES

NOTES

NOTES

NOTES